Orton Gillingham Decodable Readers

Easy decodable texts to improve reading and writing skills
in struggling readers and kids with dyslexia

Volume 3

Rebecca T. Wilkerson

Introduction

Teaching a child with dyslexia to read: Dyslexia is a specific and persistent learning disability that affects reading a writing. Teaching a child with dyslexia to read and write can become a difficult challenge for families and educato to tackle. For these children, written language becomes a great barrier, often without meaning or logic, which genera rejection of the task, frustration and discomfort.

A child with dyslexia has significant difficulties in these areas because their brain processes information different than other children, which is why if we expect the same results following the traditional method, we will find ma barriers that can and often do harm the child. It is important to become aware of the areas where the child struggles help them overcome these difficulties and make reading an easier task.

Reading difficulties with dyslexia

Dyslexia is a neurobiological disorder that affects the development and structuring of certain areas of the bra Therefore, it causes the brain to process information differently, making it difficult for the person to understand lette their sounds, their combinations, etc.

Human language is based on signs, letters and their sounds, which are arbitrary sounds. The relationship between ea grapheme (letter) with its phoneme (sound), does not follow any logic; it's simply chance. This is one of the greate difficulties that children face when they have to learn to read and write. Converting spoken language into signs a symbols, and transforming sounds into letters is a challenge. This is even more complicated in children with dyslexi the relationship becomes something indecipherable for them. No matter how hard they try, they cannot make sense that dance between letters and sounds.

Children with dyslexia have trouble recognizing letters, sometimes they mistake letters for others, write the backwards etc. They also have a hard time knowing the sound that corresponds to each letter; and things get even mo complicated when we combine several letters and we have to know several sounds. Learning new words is also challenge and they can easily forget them, so it's important that the child works hard to acquire them. Sometimes the read certain words effortlessly, but the next day they completely forget them. When they write, they omit letters, chang their position, forget words in a sentence, etc.

Dyslexia also affects reading comprehension. When reading, they are trying really hard to decipher and understan each word, sometimes even each letter; that is why the meaning of the text gets lost.

Activities to help develop reading comprehension in children

How to teach a child with dyslexia to read:

A child with dyslexia has difficulty learning to read and write because it is hard for them to recognize letters and kno which sound they correspond to. However, the child can learn to overcome those difficulties. Remember that dyslexi is a learning difficulty that does not imply any physical or mental handicap; the child with dyslexia has adequat capacities. In order to teach a child with dyslexia to read, it is essential to know the nature of their difficu understand them and use a teaching method that responds to their needs.

A teaching method to help the child read:

In the first place, it is necessary to assess the child's reading and writing level and the nature and characteristics of their difficulties, so as to understand their specific needs. For this, it's advisable to seek a specialist. Reading favors the development of phonological awareness (which consists of the letter-sound correspondence). To do this, start with simple activities, letter by letter, even if other children around the same age read full texts. Later, we can continue with full words, phrases and texts. It is about dedicating more time and more detail to the learning process.

Phonological awareness worksheets

Use motivational activities that are engaging. Do not limit the child to just paper and pencil: they can make letters out of play dough, write on sand with their fingers, play catch or games such as hangman, word searches, crossword puzzles, etc. Don't force them to read or read a lot. Try to have them read on a daily basis, little by little; sometimes a sentence or a paragraph is enough. Help them understand what they read, ask them questions, ask them to read again, etc.

TABLE OF CONTENTS

Read the story. Identify and underline all the 'lk' words.   'lk'

Walker Talks

Walker is one year old; he is Walter's younger brother. He can talk and walk. If Walker feels hungry, he says, "I want milk." For breakfast, his mother offers him an egg with a slice of bread. Walker does not eat egg yolk. He says, "I like to eat eggs, but I don't like the yolk. Can you fetch me a glass of milk?" His mother gives him a glass of lukewarm milk. He finishes his breakfast and walks towards the bathroom to wash his hands and face.

Write all the 'lk' words that you have found in the story.				

Read the story and fill in the blank
spaces with the appropriate words.

lk

Walker Talks

Walker is one year old; he is Walter's younger brother. He can _____ and _____. If Walker feels hungry, he says, "I want _____." For breakfast, his mother offers him an egg with a slice of bread. Walker does not eat egg _____. He says, "I like to eat eggs, but I don't like the _____. Can you fetch me a glass of _____?" His mother gives him a glass of lukewarm milk. He finishes his breakfast and _____s towards the bathroom to wash his hands and face.

Write any ten 'lk' words.				

Read the story and circle whether the statement is true or false. If the statement is false, provide the correct answer for it.

Walker is Walter's younger brother.

> True   False

_____
_____

Walker cannot talk but he can walk.

> True   False

_____
_____

His mother offers him an egg with two slices of bread for breakfast.

> True   False

_____
_____

Walker asked, "Can you fetch me a glass of water?"

> True   False

_____
_____

Walter walks towards the bathroom to wash his hands and face.

_____
_____

Read the story 'Walker Talks' and answer the following questions.

Who is Walker?

_____

_____

Who is Walter?

_____

_____

How old is Walker?

_____

_____

What does Walker say when he is hungry?

_____

_____

_____

Write the name of the food that Walker does not like to eat.

_____

_____

_____

Assess your reading fluency by writing the number of words read per minute.

'lk'

Walker is one year old; he is Walter's younger brother.

He can talk and walk.

If Walker feels hungry, he says, "I want milk."

For breakfast, his mother offers him an egg with a slice of bread.

Walker does not eat egg yolk.

He says, "I like to eat eggs, but I don't like the yolk.

Can you fetch me a glass of milk?"

His mother gives him a glass of lukewarm milk.

He finishes his breakfast and walks towards the bathroom to wash his hands and face.

| 10 |
| 15 |
| 24 |
| 37 |
| 43 |
| 56 |
| 64 |
| 73 |
| 88 |

Date			
Words per minute			
Number of Errors			

Read the story. Identify and underline all the 'lk' words.

lk

Words to read and highlight			
Faulk	chalk	folks	hulk
sidewalk	silk	bulk	walk

Faulk and the folks

Faulk was on her way to the shop. Faulk had to buy chalks in bulk. Faulk was walking on the road when she felt someone was stalking her. She looked back and saw some folks walking behind her. They were six-foot men that looked like the hulk. She stopped walking for a while on the sidewalk; they stopped too. Faulk was sulking and wanted to run; she started walking briskly and reached the shop. She waited for the folks to leave. Faulk bought a box of chalks and a red silk scarf.

Write all the 'lk' words that you have found in the story.

Read the story 'Faulk and the Folks' and fill in the blank spaces with the appropriate words.

lk

Point and say the sounds.				
sh	ck	lk	rk	nk
nt	ch	mp	ld	sk

Faulk and the Folks

_____ was on her way to the shop. Faulk had to buy _____s in _____. Faulk was walking on the road when she felt someone was _____ing her. She looked back and saw some _____s walking behind her. They were six-foot men that looked like the _____. She stopped walking for a while on the sidewalk; they stopped too. Faulk was _____ing and wanted to run; she started _____ing briskly and reached the shop. She waited for the folks to leave. Faulk bought a box of chalks and a red _____ scarf.

The teacher will dictate some words and the students will write them below.

_____   _____   _____

_____   _____   _____

7

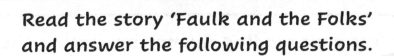

Read the story 'Faulk and the Folks' and answer the following questions.

Where was Faulk going?

_____

_____

Who was following Faulk?

_____

_____

_____

_____

What did the folks look like?

_____

_____

_____

_____

What happened when Faulk reach the shop?

_____

_____

_____

_____

_____

_____

Assess your reading fluency by writing the number of words read per minute.

Faulk was on her way to the shop.	8
Faulk had to buy chalks in bulk.	15
Faulk was walking on the road when she felt someone was stalking her.	28
She looked back and saw some folks walking behind her.	38
They were six-foot men that looked like the hulk.	47
She stopped walking for a while on the sidewalk; the folk stopped too.	60
Faulk was sulking and wanted to run; she started walking briskly and reached the shop.	75
She waited for the folks to leave.	82
Faulk bought a box of chalks and a red silk scarf.	93

Date			
Words per minute			
Number of Errors			

Write the name of each picture and listen to the ending sound. Circle 'ck' or 'lk'.

lk

ck lk	ck lk	ck lk
_____	_____	_____
ck lk	ck lk	ck lk
_____	_____	_____
ck lk	ck lk	ck lk
Hello. How are you?		
_____	_____	_____

Make sentences using the words written below.

lk

Elk

Walk

Talk

Hulk

Chalk

Bulk

Sulk

Yolk

Milk

Silk

Stalk

Find and circle the words written below.

lk

chalk   talk   walk

sulk   hulk

yolk   stalk   milk

s	h	y	o	l	k	x	p
u	c	d	e	c	k	s	w
l	g	h	w	h	i	t	a
k	h	e	a	t	v	a	l
o	w	h	y	l	n	l	k
c	p	t	a	l	k	k	e
k	f	j	m	i	l	k	l
e	h	u	l	k	m	w	k

Write a story using any five
words from the word bank.

lk

Milk   silk   talk   stalk   bulk
chalk   walk   yolk   folk   sulk
hulk   beanstalk   elk

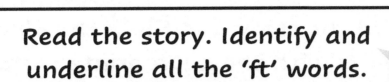

Read the story. Identify and underline all the 'ft' words.

ft

The Gift

Swift was waiting for her shift to end so that she could go to the market. She wanted to buy a gift for her friend's birthday and make her a card. She made a first draft before the final draft. Swift looked at the watch and saw that her shift was over. Swift put the draft in the left drawer and locked it. Swift went to the gift shop and started looking for a gift. She saw a soft throw pillow that had "Best friends forever" written on it. Swift said to herself, "Emma will love this pillow. I should buy this as a gift".

Write all the 'ft' words that you have found in the story.				

Read the story and fill in the blank spaces with the appropriate words.

shift	left	gift
draft	Swift	soft

The Gift

Swift was waiting for her _____ to end so that she could go to the market. She wanted to buy a _____ for her friend's birthday and make her a card. She made a first _____ before the final _____. Swift looked at the watch and saw that her _____ was over. Swift put the draft in the _____ drawer and locked it. Swift went to the _____ shop and started looking for a _____. She saw a _____ throw pillow that had "Best friends forever" written on it. _____ said to herself, "Emma will love this pillow. I should buy this as a _____".

Read the story and circle whether the statement is true or false. If the statement is false, provide the correct answer for it.

ft

Swift was waiting for her shift to end so that she could go to the hospital.

True   False

_____
_____
_____

She made a first draft before the final draft.

True   False

_____
_____

Swift put the draft in the right drawer and locked it.

True   False

_____
_____

Swift went to the gift shop and started looking for Emma.

True   False

_____
_____

Cindy will love this soft pillow.

_____
_____

16

Read the story 'The Gift' and answer the following questions.

ft

What was Swift working on?

What was Swift waiting for?

Swift was working on something. Can you write its name?

Where did Swift want to go?

What did Swift buy for her friend?

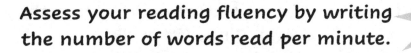

Assess your reading fluency by writing the number of words read per minute. **'ft'**

Swift was waiting for her shift to end so that she could go to the market.	16
She wanted to buy a gift for her friend's birthday and make her a card.	31
She made a first draft before the final draft.	40
Swift looked at the watch and saw that her shift was over.	52
Swift put the draft in the left drawer and locked it.	63
Swift went to the gift shop and started looking for a gift.	75
She saw a soft throw pillow that had "Best friends forever" written on it.	89
Swift said to herself, "Emma will love this pillow.	98
I should buy this as a gift".	105

Date			
Words per minute			
Number of Errors			

Write the name of each picture and listen to the ending sound. Circle 'ft' or 'lk'.

ft

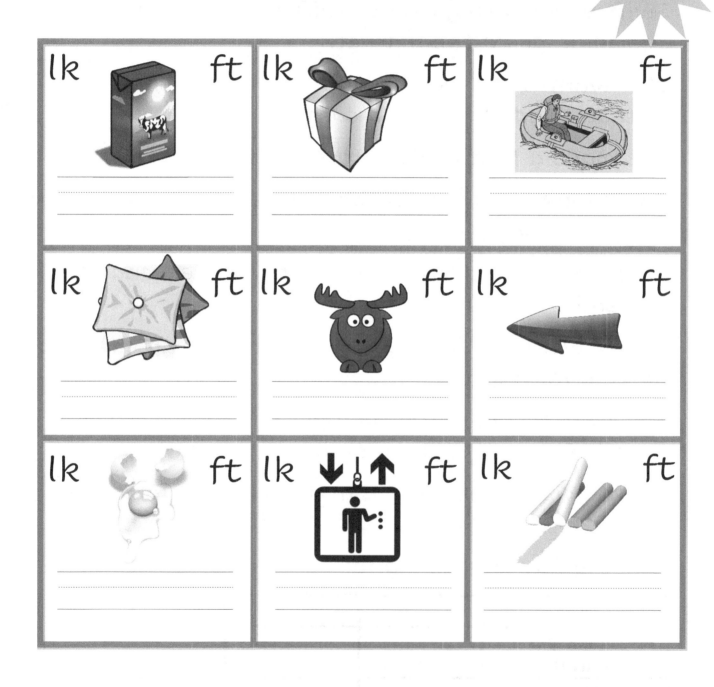

lk	ft	lk	ft	lk	ft
lk	ft	lk	ft	lk	ft
lk	ft	lk	ft	lk	ft

Make sentences using the words written below.

ft

Lift

Raft

Draft

Craft

Shift

Swift

Soft

Drift

Left

Shift

Gift

Find and circle the words written below.

ft

Lift	Gift	Drift	Draft
Soft	Left	Shift	Craft

l	e	f	t	u	x	g	b
u	i	f	k	c	k	i	a
t	d	f	n	k	i	f	n
f	h	e	t	t	v	t	k
i	d	r	i	f	t	s	k
h	c	r	a	f	t	i	i
s	f	j	s	o	f	t	n
s	d	r	a	f	t	w	k

Read the story. Identify and underline all the 'ft' words.

ft

Croft's Raft

Croft is a creative boy who is known for his craftwork. In his recent craftwork, he has made a raft. It's made out of small wooden logs. Croft installed a motor on the raft to help it drift swiftly in the water. The raft can also support some weight. Croft put a few toys on the raft to check its weight-bearing capacity. The raft started sinking towards the left side. Croft shifted the toys evenly around the four corners of the raft. Now the raft floated perfectly on the water. Croft gave his father the raft as a Father's Day gift. His father named the raft "Croft's Raft".

Write all the 'ft' words that you have found in the story.				

Read the story and fill in the blank spaces with the appropriate words.

ft

raft	Croft	drift
lift	craft	swift
shift	gift	left

Croft is a creative boy who is known for his _____work. In his recent craftwork, he has made a _____. It's made out of small wooden logs. Croft installed a motor on the _____ to help it _____ _____ly in the water. The raft can also support some weight. _____ put a few toys on the raft to check its weight-bearing capacity. The raft started sinking towards the _____ side. Croft _____ed the toys evenly around the four corners of the raft. Now the raft floated perfectly on the water. _____ gave his father the _____ as a Father's Day gift. His father named the raft "Croft's Raft".

> **Read the story and circle whether the statement is true or false. If the statement is false, provide the correct answer for it.**

Croft is a creative boy who is known for his artwork.

True   False

_____
....
_____

In his recent craftwork, he has made a car.

True   False

_____
....
_____

Croft installed batteries in the car.

True   False

_____
....
_____

Croft put a few toys on the ship to check its weight-bearing capacity.

True   False

_____
....
_____
....
_____

His father named the raft 'Father's raft.'

True   False

_____
....
_____

Read the story 'Croft's Raft' and answer the following questions.

1. What is Croft's expertise?

_____

_____

2. Can you describe how Croft made the raft?

_____

_____

_____

_____

3. What helped the raft drift swiftly in the water?

_____

_____

_____

_____

4. How did Croft check the weight-bearing capacity of the raft?

_____

_____

_____

_____

_____

_____

Assess your reading fluency by writing the number of words read per minute.

'ft'

Croft is a creative boy who is known for his craftwork.	11
In his recent craftwork, he has made a raft. It's made out of small wooden logs.	27
Croft installed a motor on the raft to help it drift swiftly in the water.	42
The raft can also support some weight.	49
Croft put a few toys on the raft to check its weight-bearing capacity.	62
The raft started sinking towards the left side.	70
Croft shifted the toys evenly around the four corners of the raft.	82
Now the raft floated perfectly on the water.	90
Croft gave his father the raft as a Father's Day gift.	101
His father named the raft "Croft's Raft".	108

Date			
Words per minute			
Number of Errors			

> Write rhyming words for the words written below.

craft			
gift			
swift			
drift			
shift			
Croft			
draft			
raft			
theft			

Make sentences using the words written below.

ft

Craft

Gift

Drift

Left

Shift

Raft

Lift

Draft

Theft

Swift

Soft

Write a story using any five words from the word bank.

ft

Soft Craft Draft Left Swift
Drift Lift Shift Raft Shaft
Gift Theft Aircraft

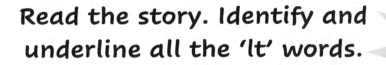

Read the story. Identify and underline all the 'lt' words.

lt

Words to read and highlight			
Belt	insult	guilt	vault
knelt	Balt	fault	quilt

Balt's Belt

Balt was getting ready for the annual St. Patrick's Day parade at school. He was almost ready to leave when he realized that he had not put on his belt. He went to his room and started looking for his belt. He looked under the quilt, but it was not there. Balt knelt to look under the bed, but also did not find it there. Balt said, "It is my fault. I should have kept it somewhere safe." Balt felt guilty and afraid of the punishment he could face for not dressing accordingly for the parade. Balt went to his mother and asked, "Can you help me find my belt?" His mother said, "I saw your belt in the vault. Have you checked there?" Balt said, "No, I will go and look for my belt in the vault." Balt found his belt in the vault.

Write all the 'lt' words that you have found in the story.

Read the story 'Balt's Belt' and fill in the blank spaces with the appropriate words.

lt

Point and say the sounds.				
sk	st	nt	nk	lt
sp	sk	nd	ct	mp

Balt was getting ready for the annual St. Patrick's Day parade at school. He was almost ready to leave when he realized that he had not put on his _____. He went to his room and started looking for his _____. He looked under the _____, but it was not there. Balt _____ to look under the bed, but also did not find it there. Balt said, "It is my _____. I should have kept it somewhere safe." Balt felt _____ and afraid of the punishment he could face for not dressing accordingly for the parade. Balt went to his mother and asked, "Can you help me find my _____?" His mother said, "I saw your belt in the _____. Have you checked there?" Balt said, "No, I will go and look for my belt in the _____." _____ found his belt in the vault.

The teacher will dictate some words and the students will write them below.		

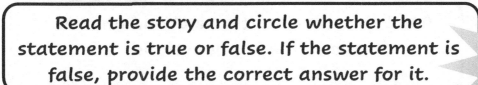

Read the story and circle whether the statement is true or false. If the statement is false, provide the correct answer for it.

lt

Balt was getting ready for the annual St. Patrick's Day parade at school.

True   False

_____

He went to his room and started looking for his belt.

True   False

_____

Balt knelt to look under the bed.

True   False

_____

"Can you help me find my belt?"

True   False

_____

Balt found his belt in the vault.

True   False

_____

"It is my fault. I should have kept it somewhere safe."

True   False

_____

Read the story 'Balt's Belt' and answer the following questions.

lt

What was Balt getting ready for?

_____

_____

_____

Why did Balt feel guilty?

_____

_____

_____

_____

_____

_____

Write the names of the places where Balt looked for his belt.

_____

_____

_____

_____

_____

Where and how did Balt find his belt?

_____

_____

_____

_____

_____

_____

_____

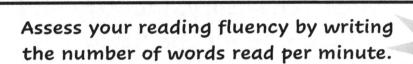

Assess your reading fluency by writing the number of words read per minute. **'It'**

Balt was getting ready for the annual St. Patrick's Day parade at school.	13
He was almost ready to leave when he realized that he had not put on his belt.	30
He went to his room and started looking for his belt.	41
He looked under the quilt, but it was not there.	51
Balt knelt to look under the bed, but also did not find it there.	65
Balt said, "It is my fault.	71
I should have kept it somewhere safe."	78
Balt felt guilty and afraid of the punishment he could face for not dressing accordingly for the parade.	96
Balt went to his mother and asked, "Can you help me find my belt?"	110
His mother said, "I saw your belt in the vault.	120
Have you checked there?"	124
Balt said, "No, I will go and look for my belt in the vault."	138
Balt found his belt in the vault.	145

Date			
Words per minute			
Number of Errors			

34

Read the story. Identify and underline all the 'lt' words.

lt

Melted Butter

Sam was having dinner with his family. He asked his little sister, "Can you pass me the salt?" Sam's sister passed him the salt and asked, "Did you gently melt the butter over low heat?" Sam said, "Yes, I melted the butter and it smelt great." Sam felt good about his cooking. Mother asked Sam, "Don't you find it difficult to cook?" Sam replied, "No, not at all. I am an adult now and I can cook. I have also made this salad tower." His mother appreciated his talents and said, "It looks lovely."

Write all the 'lt' words that you have found in the story.

Read the story 'Melted Butter' and fill in the blank spaces with the appropriate words.

lt

Point and say the sounds.				
sp	mp	ct	rp	rt
nt	sk	lt	rn	mb

Sam was having dinner with his family. He asked his little sister, "Can you pass me the _____?" Sam's sister passed him the _____ and asked, "Did you gently _____ the butter over low heat?" Sam said, "Yes, I _____ed the butter and it _____ great." Sam _____ good about his cooking. Mother asked Sam, "Don't you find it difficult to cook?" Sam replied, "No, not at all. I am an _____ now and I can cook. I have also made this salad tower." His mother appreciated his talents and said, "It looks lovely."

The teacher will dictate some words and the students will write them below.

Read the story and circle whether the statement is true or false. If the statement is false, provide the correct answer for it.

Sam was having dinner with his friends.

True   False

_____

_____

Samantha said, "I have also made this salad tower."

True   False

_____

_____

His mother appreciated his talents and said, "It looks amazing."

True   False

_____

_____

_____

_____

Sam's sister passed him the butter.

True   False

_____

_____

Sam replied, "No, not at all. I am an adult now and I can cook.

True   False

_____

_____

3

Read the story 'Melted butter' and answer the following questions.

What was Sam doing?

_____

_____

_____

What did Sam's sister ask her brother?

_____

_____

_____

_____

What did Sam's mother ask Sam?

_____

_____

_____

_____

What did Sam tell his mother?

_____

_____

_____

_____

Assess your reading fluency by writing
the number of words read per minute.

'It'

Sam was having dinner with his family.	7
He asked his little sister, "Can you pass me the salt?"	18
Sam's sister passed him the salt and asked, "Did you gently melt the butter over low heat?"	35
Sam said, "Yes, I melted the butter and it smelt great."	46
Sam felt good about his cooking.	52
Mother asked Sam, "Don't you find it difficult to cook?"	62
Sam replied, "No, not at all. I am an adult now and I can cook.	77
I have also made this salad tower."	84
His mother appreciated his talents and said, "It looks lovely."	94

Date			
Words per minute			
Number of Errors			

Write the name of each picture and listen to the ending sound. Circle 'ft' or 'lt'.

lt

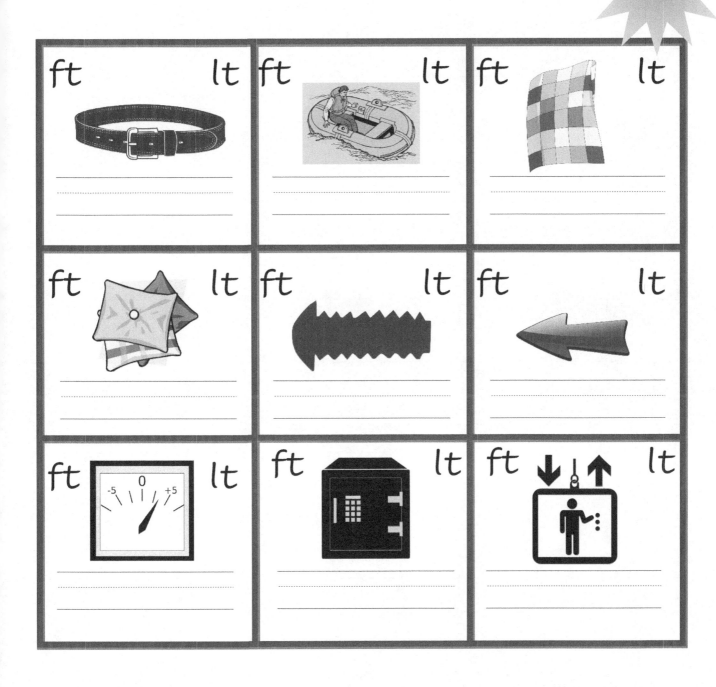

ft   lt

ft   lt

ft   lt

ft   lt

ft   lt

ft   lt

ft   lt

ft   lt

ft   lt

Make sentences using the words written below.

lt

Belt

Vault

halt

salt

melt

bolt

dealt

quilt

knelt

volt

difficult

Write a story using any five
words from the word bank.

lt

Vault	Volt	Bolt	Salt
Dealt	Knelt	Spilt	Melt
Quilt	Guilt	Built	Difficult

Read the story. Identify and underline all the 'rt' words.

Albert's shirt

Albert is going to Egypt. He checks for his passport and other documents that he will need at the airport. Albert looked for his medical report and put it away in his travel bag. He packed his luggage and put on his imported leather jacket. Albert completed all his pending tasks because he did not want to cancel his vacation plans. He looked for his cap, which was kept above the cupboard. Albert could not reach it as he was too short and needed help getting it. He stood on a stool and got his cap. Albert lost his balance and fell. His shirt got dirt all over it. He cleaned his shirt and left for the airport.

Write all the 'rt' words you have found in the story.				

Albert's Cap

Albert is going to Egypt. He checks for his _____ and other documents that he will need at the _____. Albert looked for his medical _____ and put it away in his travel bag. He packed his luggage and put on his _____ed leather jacket. Albert completed all his pending tasks because he did not want to cancel his vacation plans. He looked for his cap, which was kept above the cupboard. Albert could not reach it as he was too _____ and needed help getting it. He stood on a stool and got his cap. Albert lost his balance and fell. His _____ got _____ all over it. He cleaned his _____ and left for the _____.

Write any ten words ending with 'rt'.				

rt

Albert is going to Egypt.

True   False

_____
_____

Albert completed all his pending tasks because he did not want to cancel his vacation plans.

True   False

_____
_____
_____
_____

He stood on a box and got his cap.

True   False

_____
_____

He checks for his ID card and other documents that he will need at the airport.

True   False

_____
_____
_____
_____

Read the story 'Albert's cap' and answer the following questions.

Where was Albert going?

_____

_____

_____

_____

Why did Albert cancel completed all his pending tasks?

_____

_____

_____

_____

What happened when Albert could not find his cap? How and from where Albert finds his cap?

_____

_____

_____

_____

_____

_____

_____

Albert is going to Egypt.

| | 5 |

He checks for his passport and other documents that he will need at the airport.

| | 20 |

Albert looked for his medical report and put it away in his travel bag.

| | 34 |

He packed his luggage and put on his imported leather jacket.

| | 45 |

Albert completed all his pending tasks because he did not want to cancel his vacation plans.

| | 61 |

He looked for his cap, which was kept above the cupboard.

| | 72 |

Albert could not reach it as he was too short and needed help getting it.

| | 87 |

He stood on a stool and got his cap.

| | 96 |

Albert lost his balance and fell.

| | 102 |

His shirt got dirt all over it.

| | 109 |

He cleaned his shirt and left for the airport.

| | 118 |

Date			
Words per minute			
Number of Errors			

Read the story. Identify and underline all the 'rt' words.

rt

Hart goes shopping

Hart goes to the mart. She looks at all the beautiful clothes. She looks at a shirt with little hearts embroidered on it. Hart placed the shirt in her shopping cart. She looked for the skirts. Hart's eyes fixated on a beautiful printed short skirt. It had a digital print of a fort on it. She placed the skirt in her shopping cart. She bought five shirts and three skirts. Hart sorted all the clothes properly in her shopping cart. While shopping, she bumped into another person's cart and hurt her leg. She also tore a small part of her shirt. She went to the checkout, paid for her items, and left the mart.

Write all the 'rt' words that you have found in the story.

48

Read the story 'Hart goes Shopping' and fill in the blank spaces with the appropriate words.

Point and say the sounds.				
sh	wh	rt	ck	nt
mp	ch	st	mb	ph

Hart goes to the _____. She looks at all the beautiful clothes. She looks at a _____ with little _____ embroidered on it. _____ placed the _____ in her shopping _____. She looked for the _____. Hart's eyes fixated on a beautiful printed short _____. It had a digital print of a fort on it. She placed the skirt in her shopping _____. She bought five _____s and three _____. Hart _____ed all the clothes properly in her shopping cart. While shopping, she bumped into another person's _____ and _____ her leg. She also tore a small part of her shirt. She went to the checkout, paid for her items, and left the _____.

The teacher will dictate some words and the students will write them below.

> **Read the story and circle whether the statement is true or false. If the statement is false, provide the correct answer for it.**

rt

Hart goes to the shop.

True   False

_____

She placed the skirt in her shopping cart.

True   False

_____

She also tore a small part of her blanket.

True   False

_____

While shopping, she bumped into another person's car and hurt her leg.

True   False

_____

_____

She bought five shirts and seven skirts.

True   False

_____

Read the story 'Hart goes shopping' and answer the following questions.

Where did Hart go?

_____
....
_____

What did Hart buy?

_____
....
_____

_____
....
_____

How was Hart's shopping experience? Describe it in your own words.

_____
....
_____

_____
....
_____

_____
....
_____

Hart goes to the mart.	5
She looks at all the beautiful clothes.	12
She looks at a shirt with little hearts embroidered on it.	23
Hart placed the shirt in her shopping cart.	31
She looked for the skirts.	36
Hart's eyes fixated on a beautiful printed short skirt.	45
It had a digital print of a fort on it.	55
She placed the skirt in her shopping cart.	63
She bought five shirts and three skirts.	70
Hart sorted all the clothes properly in her shopping cart.	80
While shopping, she bumped into another person's cart and hurt her leg.	92
She also tore a small part of her shirt.	101
She went to the checkout, paid for her items, and left the mart.	114

Date			
Words per minute			
Number of Errors			

Write rhyming words for the
words written below.

rt

heart			
hurt			
short			
sort			
fort			
snort			
cart			
airport			

Write the name of each picture and listen to the beginning sound. Circle 'rt' or 'nk'.

rt

rt nk	rt nk	rt nk
_____	_____	_____
rt nk	rt nk	rt nk
_____	_____	_____
rt nk	rt nk	rt nk
_____	_____	_____

Write the words from the word bank in their appropriate places.

rt

Word Bank

art   part   dart   shirt

skirt   tart   short   expert

hurt   cart   snort

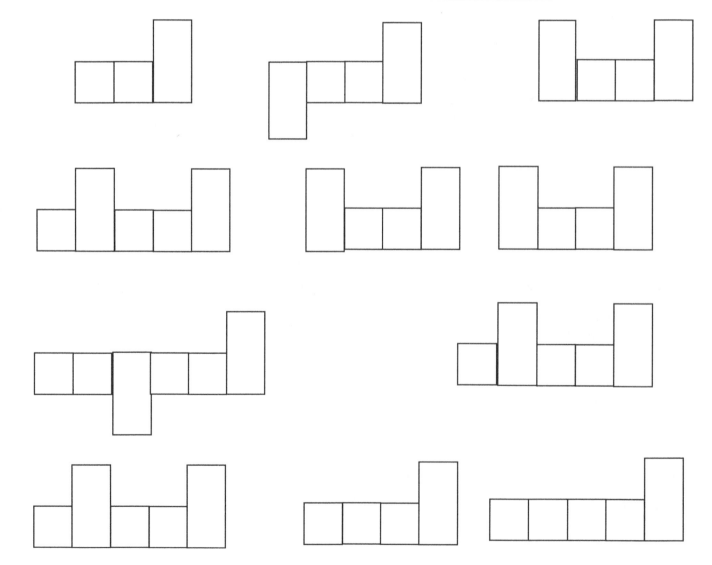

Find and circle the words written below.

Shirt   hurt   skirt   art

mart   fort   short   sort

rt

k	f	o	r	t	k	s	h
r	s	w	r	h	j	k	u
o	h	h	w	o	r	i	r
t	o	e	i	t	v	r	t
r	r	h	y	r	n	t	f
o	t	t	o	r	t	i	e
f	f	j	a	r	t	r	l
k	m	a	s	o	r	t	a

Write a story using any five words from the word bank.

rt

Shirt	hurt	yoghurt	art
Dart	snort	fort	port
airport	cart	shirt	skirt

Read the story. Identify and underline all the 'nt' words.

nt

The Ant and the Rodent

The ant and the rodent were best friends. They went exploring in the forest. They saw a tent in the middle of the forest. The ant said, "Look Mr. Rodent, what is that?" pointing towards the tent. The rodent said, "It is a tent." The tent was surrounded by beautiful plants. The ant wanted to go inside the tent and said, "I want to go inside". The ant and the rodent went inside the tent. They saw a bucket of paint and a canvas. A hydrant was painted on the canvas. The rodent bumped into the bucket and the paint spilled all over the floor. The rodent's prints were all over the floor. The rodent got scared and shouted, "Mr. Ant, let's go back. I have spilled all the paint." The ant said, "We should clean it up first". The rodent and the ant cleaned the paint and went back home.

Write all the 'nt' words that you have found in the story.				

Read the story and fill in the blank spaces with the appropriate words.

nt

The Ant and the Rodent

The _____ and the _____ were best friends. They _____ exploring in the forest. They saw a _____ in the middle of the forest. The ant said, "Look Mr. _____, what is that?" pointing towards the _____. The rodent said, "It is a tent." The tent was surrounded by beautiful _____. The ant wanted to go inside the tent and said, "I _____ to go inside". The ant and the rodent went inside the _____. They saw a bucket of _____ and a canvas. A _____ was painted on the canvas. The rodent bumped into the bucket and the _____ spilled all over the floor. The rodent's _____s were all over the floor. The rodent got scared and shouted, "Mr. Ant, let's go back. I have spilled all the _____." The ant said, "We should clean it up first". The rodent and the _____ cleaned the _____ and went back home..

Write any ten words ending with 'nt'.				

Read the story and circle whether the statement is true or false. If the statement is false, provide the correct answer for it.

nt

The ant and the rodent were best friends.

True   False

_____

_____

They went to the forest to explore.

True   False

_____

_____

The rodent's prints were all over the floor.

True   False

_____

_____

They saw a bucket of paint and a canvas.

True   False

_____

_____

The rodent and the ant cleaned the paint and went back home.

True   False

_____

_____

_____

Read the story 'The Ant and the Rodent' and answer the following questions.

nt

Who is rodent's best friend?

_____
_____
_____
_____
_____

What did they see in the middle of the forest?

_____
_____
_____
_____
_____

Can you describe the rodent's and the ant's experience? What happened inside the tent?

_____
_____
_____
_____
_____
_____
_____
_____

Assess your reading fluency by writing the number of words read per minute.

'nt'

The ant and the rodent were best friends.	8
They went exploring in the forest.	14
They saw a tent in the middle of the forest.	24
The ant said, "Look Mr. Rodent, what is that?" pointing towards the tent.	37
The rodent said, "It is a tent."	44
The tent was surrounded by beautiful plants.	51
The ant wanted to go inside the tent and said, "I want to go inside".	66
The ant and the rodent went inside the tent.	75
They saw a bucket of paint and a canvas.	84
A hydrant was painted on the canvas.	91
The rodent bumped into the bucket and the paint spilled all over the floor.	105
The rodent's prints were all over the floor.	113
The rodent got scared and shouted, "Mr. Ant, let's go back.	124
I have spilled all the paint."	130
The ant said, "We should clean it up first".	139
The rodent and the ant cleaned the paint and went back home.	151

Date			
Words per minute			
Number of Errors			

Treasure Hunt

Brant said to his friend, "Let's play treasure hunt." Brant's friend John said, "Yes, let's play treasure hunt!" Brant said, "I have hidden a few clues around the house." Brant handed John a piece of paper. "Find me at a place where all your cents are kept." John read the riddle and started running towards the piggybank. He knew that Brant kept all his cents in a piggy bank. He found the second hint underneath the piggy bank. "I point you towards a colorful place that takes you to a world of art." John ran towards the paint corner and found the third clue placed on the table. "Look closely; here, you will find a giant." John looked around and found a painting of a huge giant old age man. He looked behind the painting and found a card that had "You won" written on it.

Write all the 'nt' words that you have found in the story.

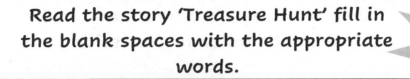

Point and say the sounds.				
nt	wh	rd	ph	nd
nk	nt	st	ch	sh

Brant said to his friend, "Let's play treasure _____." Brant's friend John said, "Yes, let's play treasure hunt!" Brant said, "I have hidden a few clues around the house." Brant handed John a piece of paper. "Find me at a place where all your _____s are kept." John read the riddle and started running towards the _____. He knew that Brant kept all his cents in a piggy bank. He found the second _____ underneath the piggy bank. "I point you towards a colorful place that takes you to a world of art." John ran towards the _____ corner and found the third clue placed on the table. "Look closely; here, you will find a _____." John looked around and found a painting of a huge _____ old age man. He looked behind the painting and found a card that had "You won" written on it.

The teacher will dictate some words and the students will write them below.

> **Read the story 'Treasure hunt' and answer the following questions.**

Write the names of the boys from the story.

_____

_____

What did Brant say to John?

_____

_____

_____

_____

What did John say to Brant?

_____

_____

_____

_____

Write the three clues John found while playing treasure hunt.

_____

_____

_____

_____

_____

_____

Brant said to his friend, "Let's play treasure hunt."	9
Brant's friend John said, "Yes, let's play treasure hunt!"	18
Brant said, "I have hidden a few clues around the house."	29
Brant handed John a piece of paper.	36
"Find me at a place where all your cents are kept."	47
John read the riddle and started running towards the piggybank.	57
He knew that Brant kept all his cents in a piggy bank.	69
He found the second hint underneath the piggy bank.	78
"I point you towards a colorful place that takes you to a world of art."	93
John ran towards the paint corner and found the third clue placed on the table.	108
"Look closely; here, you will find a giant."	116
John looked around and found a painting of a huge giant old age man.	130
He looked behind the painting and found a card that had "You won" written on it.	146

Date			
Words per minute			
Number of Errors			

Write rhyming words for the words written below.

nt

paint			
sent			
pant			
hunt			
sent			
faint			
plant			
blunt			

nt

nd nt	nd nt	nd nt
nd nt	nd nt	nd nt
nd nt	nd nt	nd nt

Find and circle the words written below.

Sent   pant   dent

Went   plant   hint   mint

nt

b	o	n	m	i	n	t	p
h	s	e	n	t	j	b	l
i	r	i	e	n	d	r	a
n	h	o	w	e	n	t	n
t	w	h	d	h	n	n	t
n	h	w	c	e	a	d	e
d	d	p	o	n	n	i	r
p	a	n	t	d	e	t	t

Write a story using any five words from the word bank.

nt

Paint	sent	went	pants
cent	plant	dent	bent
giant	blunt	vent	stunt

Read the story. Identify and underline all the 'st' words.

The Bird's Nest

Olive heard a bird chirping in the garden. The chirping sound came from the west. She walked as fast as she could and saw a little bird who was hurt. Olive tried her best to help the bird. She picked up the bird and made it sit on her wrist. Olive looked up and saw a bird's nest. All the other birds were chirping in the nest. It was a challenge for Olive to climb the tree. She started climbing the tree. Olive reached the nest and put the little bird inside it. When she was back on the ground, she saw that her clothes had gotten dirty. Olive didn't care, she was happy that the little bird was back in its nest.

Write all the 'st' words that you have found in the story.				

Read the story and fill in the blank spaces with the appropriate words.

The Bird's Nest

Olive heard a bird chirping in the garden. The chirping sound came from the _____. She walked as _____ as she could and saw a little bird who was hurt. Olive tried her _____ to help the bird. She picked up the bird and made it sit on her _____. Olive looked up and saw a bird's _____. All the other birds were chirping in the _____. It was a challenge for Olive to climb the tree. She started climbing the tree. Olive reached the _____ and put the little bird inside it. When she was back on the ground, she saw that her clothes had gotten dirty. Olive didn't care, she was happy that the little bird was back in its _____.

Write any ten words ending with 'st'.				

> **Read the story and circle whether the statement is true or false. If the statement is false, provide the correct answer for it.**

st

Olive heard a bird chirping in the garden.

True   False

_____

She walked as fast as she could.

True   False

_____

Olive tried her best to help the bird.

True   False

_____

She started climbing the tree.

True   False

_____

Olive didn't care, she was happy that the little bird was back in the nest.

True   False

_____

Read the story 'The Bird's Nest' and answer the following questions.

st

Where did Olive hear a bird chirping?

_____

_____

_____

What happened to the bird?

_____

_____

_____

_____

_____

How did Olive help the bird?

_____

_____

_____

_____

_____

_____

_____

_____

_____

_____

_____

Assess your reading fluency by writing the number of words read per minute.

st

Olive heard a bird chirping in the garden.	8
The chirping sound came from the west.	15
She walked as fast as she could and saw a little bird who was hurt.	30
	38
Olive tried her best to help the bird.	50
She picked up the bird and made it sit on her wrist.	58
Olive looked up and saw a bird's nest.	
All the other birds were chirping in the nest.	67
It was a challenge for Olive to climb the tree.	77
She started climbing the tree.	82
Olive reached the nest and put the little bird inside it.	93
When she was back on the ground, she saw that her clothes had gotten dirty.	108
Olive didn't care, she was happy that the little bird was back in its nest.	123

Date			
Words per minute			
Number of Errors			

Read the story. Identify and underline all the 'st' words.

st

The Test

It was the day of the English Grammar Test. The teacher asked the students, "Are you ready for the test? The topic for today's test is professions and you must write an essay on it. I want to be _____ when I grow up." All the students started writing. Alex wanted to be a dentist. Sam wanted to be an artist. Samantha wanted to be a scientist. Cindy was lost and did not know what she wanted to be. She made a fist and hit the desk. The teacher saw Cindy and walked over to where she was sitting. He said, "Are you alright Cindy?" Cindy said, "I am fine Mr. Brown. I don't know what I want to be." Mr. Brown said, "What do you like to do?" Cindy said, "I like to write stories, I have written a few about ghosts, treasure chests, lost children, and a life vest." Mr. Brown said, "It means you want to be a writer." Cindy asked, "Is that a profession?" Mr. Brown nodded his head yes. Cindy wrote the essay and scored the highest mark.

Write all the 'st' words that you have found in the story.

Read the story 'The Test' and fill in the blank spaces with the appropriate words.

st

Point and say the sounds.				
sh	wr	nk	ck	rt
st	ch	mp	nt	ph

It was the day of the English Grammar _____. The teacher asked the students, "Are you ready for the test? The topic for today's test is professions and you _____ write an essay on it. I want to be _____ when I grow up." All the students started writing. Alex wanted to be a _____. Sam wanted to be an _____. Samantha wanted to be a _____. Cindy was lost and did not know what she wanted to be. She made a _____ and hit the desk. The teacher saw Cindy and walked over to where she was sitting. He said, "Are you alright Cindy?" Cindy said, "I am fine Mr. Brown. I don't know what I want to be." Mr. Brown said, "What do you like to do?" Cindy said, "I like to write stories, I have written a few about _____, treasure _____, _____ children, and a life _____." Mr. Brown said, "It means you want to be a writer." Cindy asked, "Is that a profession?" Mr. Brown nodded his head yes. Cindy wrote the essay and scored the _____ mark.

The teacher will dictate some words and the students will write them below.

Read the story 'The Test' and answer
the following questions.

st

It was the day of the science test.

Sam wanted to be a scientist.

Mr. Timothy said, "What do you like to do?"

Cindy said, "I like to write stories."

The student saw Cindy and walked over to where she was sitting. He said, "Are you alright Cindy?"

The topic for today's test is transportation.

Write rhyming words for the words written below.

st

test			
past			
chest			
first			
burst			
fist			
thirst			
lust			
cast			

Read the story 'The Test' and circle the wrong word in each sentence. Rewrite each sentence using the correct word.

What was the topic of the test?

_____
_____

What was the teacher's name?

_____
_____

What did Sam wanted to be?

_____
_____

Why was Cindy blank? What did the teacher say to Cindy?

_____
_____
_____

What kind of stories did Cindy write?

_____
_____
_____
_____
_____

It was the day of the English Grammar Test.	9
The teacher asked the students, "Are you ready for the test?	20
The topic for today's test is professions and you must write an essay on it.	35
I want to be _____ when I grow up."	44
All the students started writing.	49
Alex wanted to be a dentist.	55
Sam wanted to be an artist.	61
Samantha wanted to be a scientist.	67
Cindy was lost and did not know what she wanted to be.	79
She made a fist and hit the desk.	87
The teacher saw Cindy and walked over to where she was sitting.	99
He said, "Are you alright Cindy?" Cindy said, "I am fine Mr. Brown. I don't know what I want to be."	120
Mr. Brown said, "What do you like to do?"	129
Cindy said, "I like to write stories, I have written a few about ghosts, treasure chests, lost children, and a life vest."	151
Mr. Brown said, "It means you want to be a writer."	162
Cindy asked, "Is that a profession?"	168
Mr. Brown nodded his head yes.	174
Cindy wrote the essay and scored the highest mark.	183

Date			
Words per minute			
Number of Errors			

Say the name of each picture and listen to the beginning sound. Circle 'st' or 'nd'.

st

nd st	nd st	nd st
nd st	nd st	nd st
nd st	nd st	nd st

Find and circle the words written below.

Vest   test   best   nest

Thirst   lust   crust   dust

st

v	r	w	t	e	s	t	k
b	e	w	r	h	j	s	l
d	l	s	w	h	d	e	n
u	u	e	t	r	v	b	e
s	s	h	a	k	n	n	r
t	t	e	c	r	u	s	t
n	e	t	h	i	r	s	t
e	l	e	o	p	a	r	d

Write a story using any five words from the word bank.

st

Crust	test	nest	lust	burst
thirst	first	last	most	best
fast	cast	vest	fast	west

Find and circle the words written below.

trust   point   bird   belt

curd   dirt   felt

p	o	i	n	t	h	s	r
r	r	w	o	h	j	t	o
m	o	t	r	d	i	r	t
s	h	e	k	t	v	u	f
b	o	n	d	e	n	s	e
i	b	e	l	t	l	t	l
r	m	a	r	k	k	e	t
d	x	k	c	u	r	d	k

Find and circle the words written below.

Bulk   left   felt

Sulk   theft   built

w	f	e	l	t	h	s	r
r	l	e	f	t	d	k	k
d	o	c	o	r	l	o	c
r	h	e	k	u	v	g	k
i	t	h	e	f	t	n	k
s	u	l	k	j	l	i	l
k	s	b	u	i	l	t	e
e	x	k	p	o	r	k	l

Find and circle the words written below.

Knelt   soft   fault   draft

Melt   Lift   shift

w	s	o	f	t	h	s	r
r	l	s	h	i	f	t	k
d	o	c	o	r	l	a	c
r	k	n	e	l	t	u	l
i	t	h	e	f	t	l	i
s	u	o	m	e	l	t	f
k	k	o	u	i	l	t	t
e	s	d	r	a	f	t	l

lk

Walker Talks

Walker is one year old; he is Walter's younger brother. He can talk and walk. If Walker feels hungry, he says, "I want milk." For breakfast, his mother offers him an egg with a slice of bread. Walker does not eat egg yolk. He says, "I like to eat eggs, but I don't like the yolk. Can you fetch me a glass of milk?" His mother gives him a glass of lukewarm milk. He finishes his breakfast and walks towards the bathroom to wash his hands and face.

Faulk and the folks

Faulk was on her way to the shop. Faulk had to buy chalks in bulk. Faulk was walking on the road when she felt someone was stalking her. She looked back and saw some folks walking behind her. They were six-foot men that looked like the hulk. She stopped walking for a while on the sidewalk; they stopped too. Faulk was sulking and wanted to run; she started walking briskly and reached the shop. She waited for the folks to leave. Faulk bought a box of chalks and a red silk scarf.

ft

The Gift

Swift was waiting for her shift to end so that she could go to the market. She wanted to buy a gift for her friend's birthday and make her a card. She made a first draft before the final draft. Swift looked at the watch and saw that her shift was over. Swift put the draft in the left drawer and locked it. Swift went to the gift shop and started looking for a gift. She saw a soft throw pillow that had "Best friends forever" written on it. Swift said to herself, "Emma will love this pillow. I should buy this as a gift".

Croft's Raft

Croft is a creative boy who is known for his craftwork. In his recent craftwork, he has made a raft. It's made out of small wooden logs. Croft installed a motor on the raft to help it drift swiftly in the water. The raft can also support some weight. Croft put a few toys on the raft to check its weight-bearing capacity. The raft started sinking towards the left side. Croft shifted the toys evenly around the four corners of the raft. Now the raft floated perfectly on the water. Croft gave his father the raft as a Father's Day gift. His father named the raft "Croft's Raft".

Balt's Belt

Balt was getting ready for the annual St. Patrick's Day parade at school. He was almost ready to leave when he realized that he had not put on his belt. He went to his room and started looking for his belt. He looked under the quilt, but it was not there. Balt knelt to look under the bed, but also did not find it there. Balt said, "It is my fault. I should have kept it somewhere safe." Balt felt guilty and afraid of the punishment he could face for not dressing accordingly for the parade. Balt went to his mother and asked, "Can you help me find my belt?" His mother said, "I saw your belt in the vault. Have you checked there?" Balt said, "No, I will go and look for my belt in the vault." Balt found his belt in the vault.

Melted Butter

Sam was having dinner with his family. He asked his little sister, "Can you pass me the salt?" Sam's sister passed him the salt and asked, "Did you gently melt the butter over low heat?" Sam said, "Yes, I melted the butter and it smelt great." Sam felt good about his cooking. Mother asked Sam, "Don't you find it difficult to cook?" Sam replied, "No, not at all. I am an adult now and I can cook. I have also made this salad tower." His mother appreciated his talents and said, "It looks lovely."

rt

Albert's shirt

Albert is going to Egypt. He checks for his passport and other documents that he will need at the airport. Albert looked for his medical report and put it away in his travel bag. He packed his luggage and put on his imported leather jacket. Albert completed all his pending tasks because he did not want to cancel his vacation plans. He looked for his cap, which was kept above the cupboard. Albert could not reach it as he was too short and needed help getting it. He stood on a stool and got his cap. Albert lost his balance and fell. His shirt got dirt all over it. He cleaned his shirt and left for the airport.

Hart goes shopping

Hart goes to the mart. She looks at all the beautiful clothes. She looks at a shirt with little hearts embroidered on it. Hart placed the shirt in her shopping cart. She looked for the skirts. Hart's eyes fixated on a beautiful printed short skirt. It had a digital print of a fort on it. She placed the skirt in her shopping cart. She bought five shirts and three skirts. Hart sorted all the clothes properly in her shopping cart. While shopping, she bumped into another person's cart and hurt her leg. She also tore a small part of her shirt. She went to the checkout, paid for her items, and left the mart.

Rodent and Ant

The ant and the rodent were best friends. They went exploring in the forest. They saw a tent in the middle of the forest. The ant said, "Look Mr. Rodent, what is that?" pointing towards the tent. The rodent said, "It is a tent." The tent was surrounded by beautiful plants. The ant wanted to go inside the tent and said, "I want to go inside". The ant and the rodent went inside the tent. They saw a bucket of paint and a canvas. A hydrant was painted on the canvas. The rodent bumped into the bucket and the paint spilled all over the floor. The rodent's prints were all over the floor. The rodent got scared and shouted, "Mr. Ant, let's go back. I have spilled all the paint." The ant said, "We should clean it up first". The rodent and the ant cleaned the paint and went back home.

Treasure Hunt

Brant said to his friend, "Let's play treasure hunt." Brant's friend John said, "Yes, let's play treasure hunt!" Brant said, "I have hidden a few clues around the house." Brant handed John a piece of paper. "Find me at a place where all your cents are kept." John read the riddle and started running towards the piggybank. He knew that Brant kept all his cents in a piggy bank. He found the second hint underneath the piggy bank. "I point you towards a colorful place that takes you to a world of art." John ran towards the paint corner and found the third clue placed on the table. "Look closely; here, you will find a giant." John looked around and found a painting of a huge giant old age man. He looked behind the painting and found a card that had "You won" written on it.

st

The Bird's Nest

Olive heard a bird chirping in the garden. The chirping sound came from the west. She walked as fast as she could and saw a little bird who was hurt. Olive tried her best to help the bird. She picked up the bird and made it sit on her wrist. Olive looked up and saw a bird's nest. All the other birds were chirping in the nest. It was a challenge for Olive to climb the tree. She started climbing the tree. Olive reached the nest and put the little bird inside it. When she was back on the ground, she saw that her clothes had gotten dirty. Olive didn't care, she was happy that the little bird was back in its nest.

The Test

It was the day of the English Grammar Test. The teacher asked the students, "Are you ready for the test? The topic for today's test is professions and you must write an essay on it. I want to be _____ when I grow up." All the students started writing. Alex wanted to be a dentist. Sam wanted to be an artist. Samantha wanted to be a scientist. Cindy was lost and did not know what she wanted to be. She made a fist and hit the desk. The teacher saw Cindy and walked over to where she was sitting. He said, "Are you alright Cindy?" Cindy said, "I am fine Mr. Brown. I don't know what I want to be." Mr. Brown said, "What do you like to do?" Cindy said, "I like to write stories, I have written a few about ghosts, treasure chests, lost children, and a life vest." Mr. Brown said, "It means you want to be a writer." Cindy asked, "Is that a profession?" Mr. Brown nodded his head yes. Cindy wrote the essay and scored the highest mark.

Made in the USA
Las Vegas, NV
17 October 2023

79239433R00066